The Ultimate Milkshake Recip

Creamy and Dreamy Homemade Milkshakes to Try

BY - Alain Duke

Copyright Notification

Table of Contents

Introduction

A milkshake is more than a thick and icy drink in front of the local drive-through. It is a cheerful drink intended for adults and kids, with a fun prep process that allows you to express your creativity. I created this recipe book to gather all of my fantastic milkshake recipes in one place and provide you with plenty of choices. Instead of serving plain ice cream, add a few ingredients and toss them in the blender to create a cheerful drink that everyone will enjoy.

My secret to preparing the best milkshakes is using high-quality vanilla ice cream. The rich flavor and creaminess are unmatched by any other cheap alternative. Also, I like to add some heavy cream for a richer flavor and creamier consistency. Are you ready to discover the other secrets I have to share with you? Let's review the recipes and teach you the basics of preparing tasty milkshakes at home!

1. Basic vanilla milkshake

The vanilla milkshake is a basic but delicious recipe to try. I like to add pure vanilla extract for extra flavor. Also, you can switch this with seeds from half a vanilla bean for more aroma.

Time: 5 minutes

Servings: 1

Ingredients

- 1 ½ cups vanilla ice cream, good quality works the best
- ½ cup whole milk
- 1 teaspoon pure vanilla extract

Instructions

Place the vanilla ice cream, milk, and pure vanilla extract into a blender.

Blend until the milkshake is smooth.

Now, you can adjust the consistency to your preference. If your milkshake is too thick, add some more milk. The ice cream is enough to bring sweetness but add a tablespoon of sugar if you want it sweeter. Blend again to combine if adding more milk and sugar.

Serve in a milkshake glass and garnish with whipped cream and sprinkles if desired.

2. Banana milkshake

The overripe banana adds sweetness to this recipe and a ton of flavor. Feel free to add sugar if you want a sweeter milkshake.

Time: 5 minutes

Servings: 1

Ingredients

- 1 ½ cups vanilla ice cream, good quality works the best
- ½ cup whole milk
- 1 teaspoon pure vanilla extract
- 1 overripe banana, chopped into chunks

Instructions

Place the vanilla ice cream, milk, banana chunks, and pure vanilla extract into a blender.

Blend until the milkshake is smooth.

Now, you can adjust the consistency to your preference. If your milkshake is too thick, add some more milk. The ice cream is enough to bring sweetness but add a tablespoon of sugar if you want it sweeter. Blend again to combine if adding more milk and sugar.

Serve in a milkshake glass and add whipped cream and chocolate shavings if desired.

3. Bourbon milkshake

The bourbon milkshake features a twist of the basic recipe, preparing a tasty milkshake option for adults. The bourbon adds a nice flavor enhanced with the vanilla bean.

Time: 5 minutes

Servings: 1

Ingredients

- 1 ½ cups vanilla ice cream, good quality works the best
- 2 tablespoons whole milk
- 2 tablespoons bourbon
- Seeds from ½ vanilla bean

Instructions

Place the vanilla ice cream, bourbon, milk, and vanilla seed into a blender.

Blend until the milkshake is smooth.

Now, you can adjust the consistency to your preference. If your milkshake is too thick, add some more milk. The ice cream is enough to bring sweetness but add a tablespoon of sugar if you want it sweeter. Blend again to combine if adding more milk and sugar.

Serve in a milkshake glass and garnish as desired.

4. No blender chocolate milkshake

This one is the perfect choice if you're looking for a milkshake recipe without a blender. If your blender is out of service or you want a quick and easy recipe, you only need to soften the ice cream at room temperature and mix it with the other ingredients.

Time: 15 minutes

Servings: 1

Ingredients

- 1 ½ cups chocolate ice cream, good quality works the best
- ½ cup whole milk
- 1 teaspoon pure vanilla extract

Instructions

Let your ice cream sit at room temperature for 10 minutes until softened. You don't want your ice cream to be completely melted but slightly softened. The time can vary depending on your home temperature.

Add the ice cream to a mixing bowl and mix it. Add the milk and vanilla extract and mix well to combine. Add more milk if the milkshake is too thick.

Serve in a milkshake glass and garnish with whipped cream and sprinkles if desired.

5. Chocolate milkshake

This recipe reveals the perfect ratio if you want a classic and rich chocolate milkshake. You also use cocoa powder as an alternative to chocolate sauce.

Time: 5 minutes

Servings: 1

Ingredients

- 1 ½ cups vanilla ice cream, good quality works the best
- ½ cup whole milk
- 3 tablespoons chocolate sauce

Instructions

Place the vanilla ice cream, chocolate sauce, and milk into a blender.

Blend until the milkshake is smooth.

Now, you can adjust the consistency to your preference. If your milkshake is too thick, add some more milk. The ice cream is enough to bring sweetness but add a tablespoon of sugar if you want it sweeter. Blend again to combine if adding more milk and sugar.

Serve in a milkshake glass and garnish as desired.

6. No ice cream milkshake

Even though ice cream is responsible for the creamy texture, you can prepare a milkshake without it. The secret is to use frozen bananas, giving sweetness and a creamy texture.

Time: 6 hours 5 minutes

Servings: 1

Ingredients

- 1 cup whole milk
- 1 overripe banana, chopped into chunks
- 1 cup ice
- 1 tablespoon sugar
- 1 teaspoon pure vanilla extract

Instructions

Chop the ripe banana into chunks and place it in a ziplock bag. Freeze overnight.

Add the frozen banana chunks, ice, milk, sugar, and vanilla to a high-speed blender. Blend until smooth.

Serve in a milkshake glass, and enjoy.

7. Peanut butter banana milkshake

The peanut butter and banana are classic flavors that work nicely in a milkshake. I like to add a heaping tablespoon of creamy peanut butter for the extra nutty flavor.

Time: 5 minutes

Servings: 1

Ingredients

- 1 cup whole milk
- 1 overripe banana, chopped into chunks
- 1 cup ice
- 1 tablespoon sugar
- 1 tablespoon creamy peanut butter
- 1 teaspoon pure vanilla extract

Instructions

Chop the ripe banana into chunks and place it in a ziplock bag. Freeze overnight.

Add the frozen banana chunks, peanut butter, ice, milk, sugar, and vanilla to a high-speed blender. Blend until smooth.

Serve in a milkshake glass, and enjoy.

8. Strawberry cheesecake milkshake

Adding a tablespoon of cream cheese brings the cheesecake vibe to your drink. You can top it with crushed biscuits for complete enjoyment.

Time: 5 minutes

Servings: 1

Ingredients

- 1 ½ cups vanilla ice cream, good quality works the best
- ½ cup whole milk
- 1 teaspoon pure vanilla extract
- ¾ cup strawberries, fresh or thawed
- 1 tablespoon unsalted cream cheese, softened

Instructions

Place the vanilla ice cream, strawberries, cream cheese, milk, and pure vanilla extract into a blender. If using fresh strawberries, make sure they are washed and hulled.

Blend until the milkshake is smooth.

The ice cream is enough to bring sweetness but add a tablespoon of sugar if you want it sweeter. Blend again to combine if adding more milk and sugar.

Serve in a milkshake glass and garnish with whipped cream and sprinkles if desired.

9. Oreo milkshake

Adding Oreo to your milkshake doesn't only add thickness but also enhances the flavor. The rich cocoa taste enhances your milkshake; don't forget to add more for garnishing.

Time: 5 minutes

Servings: 1

Ingredients

- 1 ½ cups vanilla ice cream, good quality works the best
- ½ cup whole milk
- 1 teaspoon pure vanilla extract
- 6 crushed Oreos
- 2 tablespoons whipped cream
- 2 crushed Oreos for garnish

Instructions

Place the vanilla ice cream, crushed Oreos, milk, and pure vanilla extract into a blender.

Blend until the milkshake is smooth.

The ice cream is enough to bring sweetness but add a tablespoon of sugar if you want it sweeter. Blend again to combine if adding more milk and sugar.

Serve in a milkshake glass and garnish with whipped cream and crushed Oreos.

10. Coffee milkshake

The simple coffee milkshake comes with three simple ingredients. But don't forget that it gives you plenty of freedom to experiment. I like to use different ingredients to alter the flavor, such as caramel syrup, chocolate syrup, and cinnamon, or add some heavy cream for a creamier drink.

Time: 5 minutes

Servings: 1

Ingredients

- 2 cups vanilla ice cream
- ¼ cup whole milk
- ¼ cup brewed coffee, cooled

Instructions

Place the vanilla ice cream, coffee, and milk into a blender.

Blend until the milkshake is smooth. Serve in a milkshake glass, and enjoy.

11. Caramel milkshake

Adding a drizzle of caramel syrup to your basic vanilla milkshake creates a decadent delight. Remember to add more on top and enjoy your delicious treat.

Time: 5 minutes

Servings: 1

Ingredients

- 1 ½ cups vanilla ice cream, good quality works the best
- 3 tablespoons whole milk
- 1 tablespoon heavy cream
- 3 tablespoons caramel sauce, homemade or store-bought

Instructions

Add the blend of ice cream, milk, heavy cream, and caramel sauce. Blend until the milkshake is smooth. The milkshake will be thicker because of heavy cream, but you can add more milk for a thinner texture.

Serve in a milkshake glass and drizzle more caramel sauce on top.

12. Chocolate PB milkshake

Chocolate and peanut butter is an excellent combination that works well. I like adding unsweetened cocoa powder to keep the rich chocolatey flavor.

Time: 5 minutes

Servings: 1

Ingredients

- 1 ½ cups vanilla ice cream, good quality works the best
- ½ cup whole milk
- 2 tablespoons creamy peanut butter
- 1 tablespoon unsweetened cocoa powder

Instructions

Place the vanilla ice cream, peanut butter, cocoa powder, and milk into a blender.

Blend until the milkshake is smooth.

Now, you can adjust the consistency to your preference. If your milkshake is too thick, add some more milk. The ice cream is enough to bring sweetness but add a tablespoon of sugar if you want it sweeter. Blend again to combine if adding more milk and sugar.

Serve in a milkshake glass, garnish with whipped cream, and sprinkle some cocoa powder on top if desired.

13. Raspberry milkshake

Raspberries have a rich berry flavor, so adding them to a milkshake creates a beautiful delight. You can use frozen raspberries, but in this case, the milkshake will be thicker.

Time: 5 minutes

Servings: 1

Ingredients

- 1 ½ cups vanilla ice cream, good quality works the best
- ½ cup whole milk
- ½ cup raspberries

Instructions

Place the vanilla ice cream, milk, and raspberries into a blender. You can use frozen raspberries for the milkshake for a thicker texture.

Blend until the milkshake is smooth.

Now, you can adjust the consistency to your preference. If your milkshake is too thick, add some more milk. The ice cream is enough to bring sweetness but add a tablespoon of sugar if you want it sweeter. Blend again to combine if adding more milk and sugar.

Serve in a milkshake glass and garnish with whipped cream and a raspberry on top if desired.

14. Blueberry lemon milkshake

The blueberry-lemon combination freshens up the creamy vanilla ice cream. The lemon zest elevates the flavor, and the vanilla extract strengthens the creamy dessert note.

Time: 5 minutes

Servings: 1

Ingredients

- 1 ½ cups vanilla ice cream, good quality works the best
- ½ cup whole milk
- 1 teaspoon pure vanilla extract
- ½ cup fresh blueberries
- 1 teaspoon lemon zest

Instructions

Place the vanilla ice cream, milk, blueberries, lemon zest, and pure vanilla extract into a blender.

Blend until the milkshake is smooth.

Now, you can adjust the consistency to your preference. If your milkshake is too thick, add some more milk. The ice cream is enough to bring sweetness but add a tablespoon of sugar if you want it sweeter. Blend again to combine if adding more milk and sugar.

Serve in a milkshake glass, and enjoy.

15. Pineapple milkshake

Milkshakes can work with fruit options such as berries, bananas, mango, pineapple, and cherries. This recipe uses fresh pineapple to let its tangy flavor bring a tropical note to this dessert.

Time: 5 minutes

Servings: 1

Ingredients

- 1 ½ cups vanilla ice cream, good quality works the best
- ½ cup whole milk
- 1 teaspoon pure vanilla extract
- 1 cup pineapple chunks

Instructions

Place the vanilla ice cream, milk, pineapple, and pure vanilla extract into a blender. If you prefer a thicker milkshake, you can use frozen pineapple chunks for this recipe.

Blend until the milkshake is smooth.

Serve in a milkshake glass and garnish with whipped cream and a maraschino cherry on top.

16. Mango milkshake

With milk ice cream and mango chunks, this recipe is a simple and easy one you can make with your kids. For a thicker and colder drink, you can use frozen mango chunks.

Time: 5 minutes

Servings: 1

Ingredients

- 2 cups vanilla ice cream
- ¼ cup whole milk
- 1 cup mango chunks

Instructions

Place the vanilla ice cream, milk, and pure vanilla extract into a blender. You can use frozen mango chunks if you prefer.

Blend until the milkshake is smooth.

Serve in a milkshake glass, and enjoy.

17. Coffee milkshake

The coffee milkshake is reserved for adults who want a combination of a cold, creamy drink and energizing coffee. You can play with the coffee amount to adjust the milkshake.

Time: 5 minutes

Servings: 1

Ingredients

- 2 cups vanilla ice cream
- ¼ cup brewed coffee, cooled
- ½ teaspoon vanilla extract
- 2 tablespoons sugar

Instructions

Place the vanilla ice cream, milk, sugar, coffee, and pure vanilla extract into a blender.

Blend until the milkshake is smooth.

Add some more sugar if desired and blend again.

Serve your milkshake with a dollop of whipped cream on top and chocolate shavings.

18. Creamy vanilla cinnamon milkshake

Adding a pinch of cinnamon makes a massive difference in the vanilla milkshake recipe. But this time, I also added some heavy cream. You can also use half and half as a substitute to bring a creamier texture.

Time: 5 minutes

Servings: 1

Ingredients

- 1 cup vanilla ice cream
- ¼ cup whole milk
- 1 tablespoon sugar
- 1 teaspoon cinnamon
- 2 tablespoons heavy cream
- ½ teaspoon pure vanilla extract

Instructions

Place the vanilla ice cream, milk, cinnamon, heavy cream, and pure vanilla extract into a blender.

Blend until the milkshake is smooth.

Serve and enjoy.

19. Pumpkin spice milkshake

The pumpkin spice milkshake is a comforting drink that will cheer you up during the fall days. I like to add some pumpkin puree and pumpkin pie spice to make this drink fall-ready.

Time: 5 minutes

Servings: 1

Ingredients

- 1 cup vanilla ice cream
- ¼ cup whole milk
- 1 teaspoon pumpkin pie spice
- ¼ cup pumpkin puree
- 1 tablespoon sugar
- ¼ teaspoon nutmeg
- 2 tablespoons heavy cream
- ½ teaspoon pure vanilla extract

Instructions

Place the vanilla ice cream, milk, pumpkin puree, pumpkin pie spice, nutmeg, and pure vanilla extract into a blender.

Blend until the milkshake is smooth.

Serve in a milkshake glass. Top with shield cream and sprinkle some pumpkin pie spice.

20. Caramel apple milkshake

The caramel apple is the right fit if you're craving more fall-inspired flavor combinations. I like adding apple pie filling and caramel sauce to achieve the perfect flavor.

Time: 5 minutes

Servings: 1

Ingredients

- 1 cup vanilla ice cream
- ¼ cup whole milk
- ¼ cup apple pie filling
- 1 tablespoon caramel sauce

Instructions

Place the vanilla ice cream, milk, and pie filling into a blender.

Blend until the milkshake is smooth.

Serve in a milkshake glass and drizzle caramel on top.

21. No ice cream milkshake

Making a milkshake without ice cream is possible. All you need to do is mix milk, heavy cream, sugar, ice cubes, and the flavor of your preference. The heavy cream adds creaminess, while the ice thickens the drink. The result is a tasty milkshake that differs from the traditional recipe that has ice cream.

Time: 5 minutes

Servings: 1

Ingredients

- 1 cup whole milk
- ½ cup heavy cream
- ½ cup icing sugar
- 1 ½ cup ice cubes
- Scraped beans from half vanilla bean
- 1 tablespoon strawberry syrup
- 2 tablespoons whipped cream

Instructions

Add the milk, heavy cream, icing sugar, ice, and vanilla beans to a blender.

Blend until the milkshake is smooth. The ice thickens the mixture, so if it looks too thick, add some more milk and blend.

Serve with whipped cream and strawberry syrup on top.

22. Coconut milkshake

This easy recipe features a creamy and tropical flavor with a mix of coconut and whole milk. Again, the ice cubes thicken the mixture, so you can add less or more to adjust it.

Time: 5 minutes

Servings: 1

Ingredients

- 1 cup whole milk
- ½ cup full-fat coconut milk
- ½ cup icing sugar
- 1 ½ cup ice cubes

Instructions

Add the milk, coconut milk, icing sugar, and ice cubes to a blender. Blend until the milkshake is smooth. The ice thickens the mixture, so if it looks too thick, add some more milk and blend.

Serve with whipped cream and coconut flakes if desired, and enjoy.

23. Red velvet milkshake

Adding red velvet cookies to your milkshake creates a thicker consistency and enriches the flavor. But also, you can try different variations of this recipe, replacing the red velvet cookies with Biscoff or Oreos.

Time: 5 minutes

Servings: 1

Ingredients

- 1 ½ cups vanilla ice cream, good quality works the best
- ½ cup whole milk
- 2 red velvet cookies
- 2 tablespoons whipped cream
- 1 tablespoon chocolate syrup
- 1 maraschino cherry

Instructions

Place the vanilla ice cream, milk, and velvet cookies into a blender.

Blend until the milkshake is smooth.

Serve in a milkshake glass and top with whipped cream, a drizzle of chocolate syrup, and a maraschino cherry.

24. Blackberry milkshake

The blackberry milkshake has an intense berry flavor and creamy texture. You can use fresh blackberries, but I always use jam instead. The jam sweetens the milkshake, but you can add some icing sugar if you like.

Time: 5 minutes

Servings: 1

Ingredients

- 1 cup whole milk
- ½ cup heavy cream
- 1 ½ cup ice cubes
- 2 tablespoons blackberry jam

Instructions

Add the milk, heavy cream, icing sugar, ice cubes, and blackberry jam to a blender. Blend until the milkshake is smooth.

Serve in milkshake glasses and garnish with whipped cream if desired.

25. Cherry milkshake

The cherry milkshake is an absolute delight for kids and adults. I like adding 1 oz of cherry brandy for the adult version for a boozy touch.

Time: 5 minutes

Servings: 1

Ingredients

- 2 cups vanilla ice cream
- ¼ cup whole milk
- 1 cup pitted cherries
- ½ teaspoon pure vanilla extract
- 2 tablespoons whipped cream
- 1 tablespoon chocolate syrup
- 1 pitted cherry for garnishing

Instructions

Place the vanilla ice cream, milk, cherries, and pure vanilla extract into a blender.

Blend until the milkshake is smooth.

Serve in a glass and garnish with whipped cream, chocolate syrup, and a cherry.

26. Cinnamon coffee milkshake

The cinnamon coffee milkshake reminds you of your favorite iced coffee from the coffee shop. I like saving money on pricey coffee and preparing this simple milkshake at home.

Time: 5 minutes

Servings: 1

Ingredients

- 1 ½ cups vanilla ice cream
- ½ cup heavy cream
- 1 teaspoon cinnamon
- ¼ cup brewed coffee, cooled
- 2 tablespoons sugar

Instructions

Place the vanilla ice cream, heavy cream, cinnamon, coffee, and sugar into a blender. Blend until the milkshake is smooth.

Serve in a milkshake glass and garnish to your preference.

27. Tiramisu milkshake

The tiramisu milkshake is an absolute delight. You can add a tablespoon of softened mascarpone cheese to the mixture, but it is optional. However, cocoa powder on top is mandatory for the ultimate experience.

Time: 5 minutes

Servings: 1

Ingredients

- 1 cup tiramisu ice cream
- ¼ cup whole milk
- 1 tablespoon mascarpone cheese, optional
- 1 tablespoon sugar
- 1 teaspoon unsweetened cocoa powder for garnishing

Instructions

Add the tiramisu ice cream, milk, sugar, and mascarpone cheese if using. Blend until combined.

Serve in a glass and sprinkle cocoa powder on top.

28. Pina colada milkshake

The delicious combination features coconut milk, pineapple, and white rum. It recreates the same flavor as the famous cocktail, coming in a creamy and icy version. For a nonalcoholic option, feel free to omit the rum.

Time: 5 minutes

Servings: 1

Ingredients

- 1 ½ cups vanilla ice cream
- ½ cup full-fat coconut milk
- 1 cup pineapple chunks
- 1 oz white rum, optional
- 2 tablespoons whipped cream
- 1 maraschino cherry
- 1 pineapple slice

Instructions

Add the vanilla ice cream, coconut milk, pineapple, and white rum if using. You can omit the rum for a nonalcoholic version of this milkshake.

Now, you can adjust the consistency to your preference. If your milkshake is too thick, add some more milk. The ice cream is enough to bring sweetness but add a tablespoon of sugar if you want it sweeter.

Serve in a glass and garnish with whipped cream, maraschino cherry, and a pineapple slice.

29. Matcha milkshake

Adding a teaspoon of matcha powder to your milkshake creates a tasty drink with plenty of energy.

Time: 5 minutes

Servings: 1

Ingredients

- 1 ½ cups vanilla ice cream, good quality works the best
- ½ cup whole milk
- 1 teaspoon matcha powder

Instructions

Add the matcha, vanilla ice cream, and whole milk to a blender. Blend until the milkshake is smooth.

Serve in a milkshake glass, and enjoy.

30. Mocha almond milkshake

The mocha almond milkshake is another recipe resembling an overpriced iced coffee. The combination of chocolate ice cream, almond butter, and coffee creates a delightful treat that doubles as a caffeine drink.

Time: 5 minutes

Servings: 1

Ingredients

- 2 cups chocolate ice cream
- ¼ cup brewed coffee, cooled
- 2 tablespoons almond butter
- ½ teaspoon vanilla extract
- 2 tablespoons chocolate syrup

Instructions

Add the chocolate ice cream, coffee, almond butter, and vanilla extract to a blender.

Blend until the milkshake is smooth.

Garnish the sides of the milkshake glass with chocolate syrup. Pour in the milkshake and drizzle some more syrup on top. Serve and enjoy.

31. Salted caramel coffee milkshake

The milkshake combination features creamy vanilla IEC cream, decadent caramel syrup, and a bit of cinnamon that adds aroma. If you don't have a salted caramel sauce, use the regular one and throw in a pinch of salt.

Time: 5 minutes

Servings: 1

Ingredients

- 2 cups vanilla ice cream
- ¼ cup brewed coffee, cooled
- 2 tablespoons salted caramel syrup
- ½ teaspoon vanilla extract
- 1 teaspoon cinnamon

Instructions

Add the vanilla ice cream, salted caramel syrup, coffee, vanilla extract, and cinnamon to a blender.

Blend until the milkshake is smooth.

Drizzle some more salted caramel up on the sides of the glass. Serve the milkshake and enjoy.

Conclusion

After checking these fabulous milkshake recipes, you learn the secrets to preparing the best. You discovered that high-quality vanilla ice cream works best in recipes with fewer ingredients. But also you learned how to add flavor and prepare tasty flavor combinations. Adding coffee and alcohol enhances the flavors, so go ahead when preparing milkshakes for adults.

Also, you learned how to prepare milkshakes without ice cream. And you knew a secret trick to prepare a milkshake without a blender. Add a handful of fresh or frozen fruits or two tablespoons of fruit jam when you want fruit-flavored milkshakes. The possibilities are endless, so that you can experiment and develop your flavors.

If you liked the milkshake recipe book, explore our endless world of recipes; you will find something that suits your preferences!

Thank You

The gratitude I feel for your purchase of my book cannot be expressed in words. Each sale shows me that individuals are benefiting from my experiences and knowledge. Becoming a writer was a decision I made because it allows me to share my skills and expertise with others.

Out of the numerous books available, you chose mine, which is extremely special to me. I have no doubt that the information presented in the book will be useful and informative for you.

Please remember to leave feedback once you've finished reading the book. Every piece of feedback, no matter how small, is invaluable to me in creating even better books. I listen carefully to my readers and take their suggestions into account when developing new content. Your honest feedback will be incorporated into my next books.

Thank you once again for your support.

Alain Duke

Printed in Great Britain
by Amazon

35663327R00040